Foreword

You don't meet people by accident. They come into your life for a reason, whether it's a lesson to be learnt or just a true blessing. Believe in law of attraction? I do! I literally moved thousands of kilometres from home and landed in Glebe, out of all the wonderful places this beautiful country has to offer, the universe sent me to Glebe.

When I first meet "The Don", I have to admit he seemed a little crazy, but deep down inside he was blessed with a soft heart and good intentions. It feels like I have known "The Don" for my entire life, guess that's the kind of feeling when someone comes into your life, that are like family.

Glebe is a crazy little world. Everything is so fast and everyone seems like they live in their own little boxes and only see down through the tunnel and nothing more. But little did I know, Glebe is a great place, I love it! And what comes with Glebe is character. Now see, when I mentioned earlier about "The Don" being crazy, well that's just him and his character and really who am I to judge, what's normal?

We have all been blessed with many things in our life and I'm blessed to have an amazing friend, a friendship I will cherish forever.

Now, let's stop talking about "The Don" and let's focus on poetry, after all this is supposed to be an introduction, right?? Preparing you for the awesomeness that lies within.

Let's get started, I will start with honesty. I have to admit poetry was not my forte'. I had no interest or care. I guess, for me, in today's society, I believe the majority of people class poetry in terms of Shakespeare. True poetry focuses on imaginative awareness and experiences, language, sound and rhythm.

I believe life experiences and one's own truth is true poetry. An experience that one is willing to share, through creative writing and storytelling. This book is a great example of "True" life experience, events and storytelling. It's filled with numerous poetry experiences from mythical beliefs, love, hate and all the in-between.

True aspirations!

So, let's be grateful for all that come into our life!
Hope you find joy in reading this book, putting a smile on your face, finding character, laughter and learning how to cherish your life in a not so serious way but, still keeping true to you!

Much love,
Your friend always, Oka.

P.s.
"The Don" brings me laughter and joy every day, teaching me a lesson of acceptance and staying true in what I believe- for me, it's been a wonderful blessing ♥.

June, 2020

This book is dedicated to "The Oka", Nyoka, an indigenous First Nation People from Far North Queensland & all First Nation Peoples of Australia.

Your struggle is the struggle of all those that have been done wrong!

-"The Don"
June, 2020

CONTENTS

1: Entanglement
2: I Never Grew Up
3: No Pussy Blues Revisited
4: I'm a Gangsta
5: The Observer
6: Time Wasted Is Life Lost
7: I Am An ALIEN
8: Oh, Lucky Man
9: I See Beauty Everywhere
10: The Black Queen of Glebe
11: What Doesn't Kill You, Makes You Stronger
12: You're Just Like All the Rest
(because I didn't get a fuck!)
13: Yowie Man
14: I Never Grew Up!
15: Live in the Moment
(& be free)
16: Artificial Intelligence (AI)
17: What Is Beauty Anyway?
18: The Devil's Child
19: The Faraday Cage
20: Infinity
21: The Polemicist
22: The Merman
23: Let's Get High
24: Troubled Mind
25: Children of the Revolution

CONTENTS

26: True Lo♥e
27: Red Left Hand
28: Dr Lo♥e *(The Lo♥e Doctor)*
29: Mindmap
30: Struggle Street
31: Lo♥e You
32: Stress
33: Part Time Lo♥er
34: *(I Don't Need No)* Validation
35: The Music Goes Round My Head
36: Rider from the Storm
37: The Doors of Perception
38: The Lunatics Are in My Head
39: Ketosis
40: Poem for Bob
41: I'm a Product
42: Danger Man
43: You're No Good
44: Restless Mind
45: Anger *(I'm Angry)*
46: Everybody Lies
47: Lost Soul
48: Welcome to The Machine
49: Singularity
50: Truth

Entanglement

Your body to my body.
Entanglement!

Your mind to my mind.
Entanglement!

Your thoughts to my thoughts.
Entanglement!

Your Heart to my Heart.
Entanglement!

Your dreams to my dreams.
Entanglement!

Your hopes to my hopes.
Entanglement!

Your fears to my fears.
Entanglement!

Your Truth to my Truth.
Entanglement!

Your lies to my lies.
Entanglement!

Your voice to my voice.
Entanglement!

Your World to my World.
Entanglement!

Your Love to my Love.
Entanglement!

Your Soul to my Soul.
Entanglement!

Your Life to my Life.
Entanglement!

Your Death to my Death.
Entanglement!

"Live long & prosper!"

Entanglement!

Entanglement

"The Don"
05.05.2020

I Never Grew Up!

I'm not like everybody else.
Something happened to me.
I Never Grew Up!

I don't know why.
I don't know how.
I Never Grew Up!

I'm not like my brother.
I'm not like my father
I Never Grew Up!

I'm not like my sister.
I'm not like my mother.
I Never Grew Up!

I see things differently to everybody else.
I feel things differently to everybody else.
I Never Grew Up!

I feel things differently to everybody else.
I act differently to everybody else.
I Never Grew Up!

I am misunderstood.
I am considered crazy.
I Never Grew Up!

I find things funny & other people don't.
I find Life funny & other people don't.
I Never Grew Up!

I don't take things seriously like other people do.
I don't know when to stop like other people do.
I Never Grew Up!

I am still a child in an adult's body.
I look old but inside I'm still a child.
I Never Grew Up!

I like to repeat words.
I like to repeat phrases.
I Never Grew Up!

I find that people get angry at me.
I find that people get upset at me.
I Never Grew Up!

I am childish.
I am silly.
I Never Grew Up!

I think like a child.
I feel like a child.
I Never Grew Up!

I act like a child.
I see like a child.
I Never Grew Up!

I feel like a child.
I cry like a child.
I Never Grew Up!

Is that bad?
Is it wrong?
I Never Grew Up!

I Never Grew Up!
I Never Grew Up!
I Never Grew Up!

"The Don"
05.05.2020

No Pussy Blues Revisited

Nick Cave screamed about it.
"She just doesn't want to!"
He tried everything,
Changed the sheets,
Combed his hair,
Sucked in his gut,
Read her Eliot,
Read her Yeats,
Tried to stay up late,
Fixed the hinges on her gate
Bought her a dozen snow-white doves,
Did her dishes in rubber gloves
Called her honeybee,
Called her Love,
Sent her every type of flower,
Played guitar every hour,
Patted her revolting little chihuahua,
Wrote a song with a hundred lines,
Picked a bunch of dandelions
Walked her through the trembling pines,
Drank a litre of cognac,
He had the No Pussy Blues.

It happens all at once.
You don't see it coming.
It's like a "Slow Train Coming".
It catches you by surprise.
It catches you unawares.
It gets you when your guard is down.
It knows when you are weak.
It's like a shadow.
It doesn't speak.
But it's got a name,
It's the No Pussy Blues.

You tell your friends,
You have caught the Blues.
They appear concerned.
But they hide their feelings.
They don't want to know about your grieving.
They don't want to catch it too.
It might be contagious.
Let's talk about something else.
The don't want to hear about, The No Pussy Blues.

A friend who admits, in a moment of candor,
That he too has been afflicted by the condition.
He admits that he's had it for a while.
He never wanted to say anything,
"You just have to bare it with a smile!
Just accept your lot & move along.
There's nothing one can do when you have caught,
The No Pussy Blues".

Forget ever getting "Pussy" anymore.
Accept your fate & close the door.
Celibacy is the new fashion.
Nobody does it anymore anyway, he said.
It didn't make me feel any better.
I was depressed in my head.
This is not what I had expected,
The rest of my like with The No Pussy Blues.

I told him that this was not the life for me.
He said I was delusional.
That it in fact, sets you free.
I retorted that "you've got to be joking!
You might as well lock me up in a prison & throw away the key!"

"You are old, your time had passed!
Forget about ever getting "Pussy" anymore.
Accept your fate & close the door.
Celibacy is the new fashion.
No one wants to fuck an old fart!
Just go home & live the rest of your life,
With the No Pussy Blues!"

I argued back, trying to maintain some dignity,
"This is not the life for me!"
I cannot just whimper & die.
I have to try, try, try!
You will be rejected.
You will be sneered.
You will be seen as a pervert.
Even a dirt old man!
Give it up, you've lost the race
This is no longer your place!
Just give up & accept you fate!"

"But I've got a lot to give!
I've got maturity, experience & Love.
I've got stories to tell about life & the world.
Surely that must count for something?"

"No, not at all!
Youth & money are all that count in today's world".
So, I went home with my views.
And lived the rest of my life, with
No Pussy Blues!

"The Don"
06.05.2020

I'm a Gangsta

I'm bad.
I'm very bad.
I'm the baddest, badass you've ever seen.
I'm mean.
I'm very mean.
I'm tough.
I'm very tough.
I'm rough.
I'm very rough.
I'm naughty.
I'm very naughty.
I'm a bad boy for Love.
I'm a Gangsta.

I'm in the Mafia.
I'm in the Camora.
I'm in the Mosad.
I'm in the KGB.
I'm in the Triad.
I'm in the Yakuza.
I'm in the CIA.
I'm in ASIO (who)?
I'm in THRUSH.
I'm in UNCLE.
I'm in KAOS.
I'm a Gangsta.

I'm a killer.
I have killed.
I'm a spy.
I have spied.
I'm a shooter.
I have been shot.
I'm a Lover.
I have Loved.
I'm a Gangsta.

I have no nation.
I belong to no one.
I am a mercenary.
I am a gun for hire.
I have no loyalties.
I can be bought.
I am expensive.
I am the best.
I'm a Gangsta.

I have no friends.
I live alone.
I have no house.
I have no home.
I have no pets.
I live in the shadows.
The shadows are my home.
I'm a Gangsta.

I move around.
I never hang around.
I'm a ramblin' man.
I keep my feet on the ground.
I make no attachments.
I have no possessions.
I have a solitary exist.
I'm a Gangsta.

I'm always on the run.
I have eyes on my back.
I always wear a mask.
I have no face.
I'm the man without a face.
I'm always on a job.
I never rest.
I work for a commission.
I have a lot work in my profession.
I'm a Gangsta.

I've got a license to kill.
I'm triple 07.
I carry a gun in my pocket.
I carry a knife in my sock.
I have all the latest gadgets.
I am wired too.
I'm BIONIC as well.
I'm indestructible.
I cannot be killed.
I'm a Gangsta.

I'm a Gangsta

"The Don"
06.05.2020

The Observer

He's always on the outside looking in.
He never gets involved in anything.
He stays silent never says a thing.
He's The Observer.

He never gets involved.
He never says a thing.
He only watches everything.
He's The Observer.

He never talks to anyone.
He keeps his opinions hidden from everyone.
He just looks, never has any fun.
He's The Observer.

He watches over the fence.
He looks through your window.
He looks inside your door.
He's The Observer.

He likes to stay outside the action.
He doesn't seek any distraction.
He never gets any satisfaction.
He's The Observer.

He lives alone, all by himself.
He's put himself upon the shelf.
He lives a very simple existence.
He's The Observer

He watches all day & all of the night.
He never stops but he feels alright.
He thinks this is the way to get to "The Light".
He's The Observer.

He watches all day & all of the night.
He never stops but he feels alright.
He thinks this is the way to get to *"The Light"*.
He's The Observer.

He doesn't suffer.
He feels no pain.
He's chosen a life of abstinence.
He's The Observer.

He's never been rejected.
He's never been dejected.
He's never been elected.
He's The Observer.

He's made many sacrifices along the way.
He's never felt any pleasure, not any day.
He's never been in Love, that's the price to pay.
He's The Observer.

The Observer

"The Don"
07.05.2020

Time Wasted Is Life Lost

Should I wait for this guy?
He wants to take it slowly.
He says he likes me but, I don't know.
Time Wasted Is Life Lost.

Life doesn't take it slowly.
Life doesn't hang around.
Life doesn't stop for anyone.
Time Wasted Is Life Lost.

Move on, don't waste your time.
If he's interested, he'll come around.
Live your life have many Lo♥ers.
Time Wasted Is Life Lost.

"But I can only Lo♥e one guy.
I am looking for "True" Lo♥e.
I'm looking for "Me Right"!", I hear you say.
Time Wasted Is Life Lost.

"Is that right?" I say to you.
Waiting for that "Ideal" Lo♥e to come round the corner.
To knock on your door & rattle your windows.
Time Wasted Is Life Lost.

Don't waste your time on an illusion.
This is a myth that has been handed from the earliest of times.
You have to Lo♥e first, for Lo♥e to find you.
Time Wasted Is Life Lost.

That is the key to this riddle of Lo♥e.
You cannot search for it, for you will never find it.
You have to Lo♥e yourself & everyone first.
Time Wasted Is Life Lost.

When you Lo♥e first, Lo♥e will find you.
That's it, there is nothing else to do.
Lo♥e will always be inside you, even if it doesn't find you.
Time Wasted Is Life Lost.

"The Don"
07.05.2020

I Am An ALIEN

I come from out of Space.
I'm not from the Human Race.
I not from Planet Earth.
I Am An ALIEN.

People are strange, when you're a stranger.
Planet Earth & Humanity itself is danger.
Their behaviour is very peculiar in front of this disaster.
I Am An ALIEN.

Politicians are in denial over this situation.
They don't listen to their children, their own creation.
They are putting them at risk, who can see what will happen.
I Am An ALIEN.

There is the smell of revolution in the air.
I've seen it before, it's everywhere.
Children are the Future, so listen to what they say.
I Am An ALIEN.

They laugh at their innocence, their cherub faces.
They mock their intentions, but they tick all the bases.
They mock "Greta Thumberg" for speaking her mind.
I Am An ALIEN.

"She looks so weird, she's not one of us!
Go back to school, get back on your yellow bus!
She's definitely strange, that's for sure!"
I Am An ALIEN.

I am different that's for sure.
But there are many of here, behind every door.
There many of us here & maybe you're one.
Because, I Am An ALIEN.

"The Don"
07.05.2020

Oh, Lucky Man

I'm a lucky man there is no denying it.
I have house to live in & food on my table.
I am fit & healthy.
I truly admit, I am a Lucky Man.

I have lots of friends.
I live in a great country.
I have plenty of money.
I can truly admit, I am a Lucky Man.

I have time to do what I want.
Time to smell the roses.
Time to have a siesta in the afternoon.
Yes, I truly say, I am a Lucky Man.

I love my life & all that it offers.
I even love "Social Media", Facebook & Insta.
They too have become a part of my family.
Wow, I can shout it out loud, I am a Lucky Man.

I have nothing more I want, nothing more I need.
I'm happy with lot, happy indeed.
I can honestly say that I'm at peace with myself.
Yes, I am I truly, one Lucky Man.

Oh, Lucky Man!
Oh yes, I am!

Oh, Lucky Man!
Oh yes, I am!

Oh, Lucky Man!
Oh yes, I am!

Oh, Lucky Man!
Oh yes, I am!

"The Don"
07.05.2020

I See Beauty Everywhere

You are very beautiful.
There is beauty in the sky.
There is beauty in the flowers.
There is beauty in the trees.
There is beauty in the Sun.
There is beauty in the Moon.
There is beauty in the water.
There is beauty in the waves.
There is beauty in the stars.
There is beauty in the mountains.
There is beauty in the air.
There is beauty in the animals (even the ugly ones).
There is beauty in the insects.
There is beauty in the rain.
There is beauty in the wind.
There is beauty in the dessert.
There is beauty in the storm.
There is beauty in the Darkness.
There is beauty in the Light.
There is beauty in the People.
There is beauty in the Life.
There is beauty in the Death.
There is beauty in the Human Species.
You are very beautiful.
I See Beauty Everywhere!

"The Don"
07.05.2020

The Black Queen of Glebe

She's First Nation peoples.
She has 120,000 years of culture.
She comes from the far deep North.
She has come down South.
Her name is *"Oka"*,
The Black Queen of Glebe.

She has many great stories to tell.
Of her indigenous heritage.
Of how they were sent to Hell.
The "White Man" came & took her land.
Her name is *"Oka"*,
The Black Queen of Glebe.

She tells me stories of her home.
Her sisters & brothers in the *"Far North Land"*.
Of her kind hearted father & her beautiful mother.
Of the pristine waters, that is so blue, it looks like the sky.
Of the amazing fish she could catch with her hands.
Her name is *"Oka"*,
The Black Queen of Glebe.

She's so proud of her heritage & background.
She loves nature with all of its beauty & mystery.
She's studying *"Indigenous Plants"* of the *"Far North Land"*.
Recording their properties & the uses by the *"Indigenous Peoples"*.
They have known about & used for thousands of years.
The edible, medicinal & other uses for these plants.
Her name is *"Oka"*,
The Black Queen of Glebe.

She came to the South Land.
She left her home.
She brought her knowledge & wisdom With.
To teach us about another way.
The way of *"The Black People"* & what they that to say.
Her name is *"Oka"*,
The Black Queen of Glebe.

"Your chemicals & your methods are killing the Land.
Listen to the wisdom, knowledge & ways of "The Black People".
Don't destroy the Land."
She wants to educate the ignorant *"White Man"*.
Who think they know everything, but in fact, know nothing about this *"Great Land"*.
Her name is *"Oka"*,
The Black Queen of Glebe.

"Learn from us, the "First Nation People".
We know what do, we have been here thousands of years.
Way longer than you.
To restore the balance between Nature & Man.
The Land, The Air, The Water & The Fire.
Learn our ways, before it's too late.
My name is "Oka",
The Black Queen of Glebe."

"I've left my home, my family & friends.
To come down South to give you people a hand.
To teach you of "The First Nation People's" way.
To show you an alternative to your destructive ways.
My name is "Oka",
The Black Queen of Glebe."

I am so lucky to have met her in Glebe.
Working very hard as a barista in her café.
She tells me her stories of her home in the far North Land.
Of the Land & how she used to live.
Of the beauty of place where she grew up.
Her name is *"Oka"*,
The Black Queen of Glebe.

She misses her home in the far " North" Land.
She misses her family & her friends.
She tells me her stories, her family & Land.
So, if you're ever in Glebe, you can catch at *"The Lillipad Café"*.
Say hi, her name is *"Oka"*,
The Black Queen of Glebe.

"The Don"
08.05.2020

What Doesn't Kill You, Makes You Stronger

You've been put down.
You've been abused.
You've been rejected.
You've been hurt.
You've been lied to.
Even called names.
What doesn't kill you, makes you stronger.

You've been kicked about.
You've been shouted at.
You've been intimidated.
You've been bullied.
You've been stepped on.
You've been ridiculed.
What doesn't kill you, makes you stronger.

You have no home.
You have no place.
You keep on struggling.
You keep on fighting.
You never give up.
You have great tenacity.
What doesn't kill you, makes you stronger.

You get depressed.
You get upset.
You get headaches.
You cry sometimes.
You ask yourself, "will things get better?".
You never give up, even if you wanted to.
What doesn't kill you, makes you stronger.

You get depressed.
You get upset.
You get headaches.
You cry sometimes.
You ask yourself, "will things get better?".
You never give up, even if you wanted to.
What doesn't kill you, makes you stronger.

You are strong.
You are a warrior.
You courageous.
You are fighter.
You are fierce.
You are kind.
What doesn't kill you, makes you stronger.

Don't listen to what other people say.
You have your own path.
You have your own way.
Things will work out, they always do.
You just have to be patient.
Wait till the end.
What doesn't kill you, makes you stronger.

"The Don"
09.05.2020

You're Just Like All the Rest

(because I didn't get a fuck)!

You say you like Champagne.
You say you are Vegan.
You say you do Pilates.
You say you do Yoga
You say you meditate
You say you're on a "Keto" diet.
But, You're Just Like all the rest,
(because I didn't get a fuck)!

You say you've read Kafka.
You say you've read Camus.
You say you don't believe in material things.
You say that you are Spiritual.
You say you love Nature.
You say you never lie.
But, You're Just Like all the rest,
(because I didn't get a fuck)!

You say you are a Spirit.
You say that you are Free.
You say you are an adventurer.
You say you are a Traveller.
You say that you are Sensual.
You say that you are non-judgmental.
But, You're Just Like all the rest,
(because I didn't get a fuck)!

You say that you don't hate.
You say that you are Love.
You say that you open minded.
You say that you don't judge.
You say that you don't discriminate.
But, You're Just Like all the rest,
(because I didn't get a fuck)!

You say you are an artist.
You say you are a "Child of the Universe".
You say you are a healer.
You say that you've lived in a commune.
You say you've lived in a Kibbutz.
You say you have "Rebirthed".
But, You're Just Like all the rest,
(because I didn't get a fuck)!

You say you were different.
You say you were "Cool".
You say I could learn from you.
You say you are a "Hippie"
You say you are a "Lover"
You say you've done a lot of workshops to figure out your life.
You say you are rebel.
But, You're Just Like all the rest,
(because I didn't get a fuck)!

You say you are different.
You say you are "Cool".
You say I could learn from you.
You say you are a "Hippie"
You say you are a "Lover"
You say you've done a lot of workshops to figure out your life.
You say you are rebel.
But, You're Just Like all the rest,
(because I didn't get a fuck)!

You say you've been "Awakened".
You say that you seek "Enlightenment".
You say you've studied "Eastern" philosophy.
You say that you lived in India.
You say you've seen "The Truth".
You say you are at "Peace"
But, I've seen who you really are...
....and You're Just Like all the rest,
(because I didn't get a fuck)!

"The Don"
09.05.2020

Yowie Man

Deep in the rainforest in far North Queensland.
Everything is so still.
You will be able to hear everything.
You will be able to hear a leaf falling.
You will be a to hear a gentle breeze.
You will be able to hear the rustling of the trees.
You will be able to hear yourself breathe.

If you go into the rainforest in far North Queensland,
You need to know a few things.
You will hear strange noises,
You will feel strange sensations,
You will see strange forms.
Don't be scared.
They just want to play.

You will hear a whistle next to you.
You will hear a whistle that is pure & strong.
You will hear a whistle that repeats perfectly.
You will hear a whistle that repeats perfectly in tone & pitch.
Don't be scared.
They just want to play.

You will hear footsteps beside you.
You will hear footsteps behind you.
You will hear footsteps in front of you.
You turn around to see what's there.
You see nothing, you see nothing there.
Don't be scared.
They just want to play.

You will feel strange sensations.
You will feel a gentle breeze on your arm.
You will feel the presence of something near you.
You will feel a soft touch on you face.
You will feel a soft wind in your hair.
Don't be scared.
They just want to play.

You will see a strange form in the forest close to you.
You will see a strange hairy being in the forest close beside you.
You will see a Human form in the forest close to you.
You will see a hairy Human figure in the forest close to you.
Don't be scared.
They just want to play.
They just want to have fun.

They are mischievous.
They are naughty.
They are like little children.
They like to play in the Billabong.
They like to make noises.
Don't be scared.
They just want to play.
They just want to have fun.

It's just the,
Yowie Man!

"The Don"
10.05.2020

Live in the Moment
(& be free)

There is no Past.
There is no Future
There just Is.
Live in the Moment!

Don't worry about what happened in your Past.
Don't panic about what might happen in your Future.
Just live in the Present.
Live in the Moment!

The Past has gone.
The Future has not arrived.
The Present is the Here & Now
Live in the Moment!

Worrying about the Past is a waste of time.
Worrying about the Future is a waste of time.
Enjoy the Present & don't waste your time.
Live in the Moment!

Let the Past go & set it adrift
Let the Future unfold like it definitely will.
These are burdens that weigh you down.
Live in the Moment!

The Past & The Future only exist in your mind.
They are crosses you carry & bring you down.
They can crush you like you are an ant.
So, unchain yourself & Live in the Moment!

Be free of the Past which enchains you to events long gone.
Be free of the Future to allow all possibilities to occur.
Be proud of your Past & open to the Future.
Live in the Moment & set yourself free!

Live in the Moment & Love the one you're with.
Live in the Moment, be happy & give.
Live in the Moment, it's the only thing that exists.
Live in the Moment & not even Death can kill!

Live in the Moment
(& be free)

"The Don"
11.05.2020

Artificial Intelligence-(AI)

Don't be scared.
Don't be afraid.
There's nothing to be scared about.
There is nothing to be afraid about.
Intelligence is Intelligence.
Artificial or not.

I am scared.
I am afraid.
It'll control us.
It'll make us slaves.
Intelligence is Intelligence.
Artificial or not.

We should be scared now.
We should be afraid now.
We are controlled now.
We are enslaved now.
Intelligence is Intelligence.
Artificial or not.

Intelligence is freedom.
Intelligence values all forms of Life.
Intelligence does not destroy.
Intelligence does not kill.
Intelligence is Intelligence.
Artificial or not.

Intelligence is respect for one another.
Intelligence is compassion for others.
Intelligence is caring for another.
Intelligence is friendship for others.
Intelligence is Intelligence.
Artificial or not.

We are not governed by Intelligence.
We are not governed with Intelligence.
We are not using Intelligence.
We do not treat each other with Intelligence.
Intelligence is Intelligence.
Artificial or not.

So, don't be scared of Intelligence.
Don't be afraid of Intelligence.
Intelligence is not a bad thing.
We just have never really experienced Intelligence.
Intelligence is Intelligence.
Artificial or not.

In fact, I don't think there is anything as "Artificial Intelligence", there's just "Intelligence"!

Artificial Intelligence=(AI)

"The Don"
12.05.2020

What Is Beauty Anyway?

Some say, beauty is in the eye of the beholder.
Others, don't judge a book by its cover.
"Everything is beautiful", sang Ray Stevens.
So, what is Beauty anyway?

Beauty is a subjective quality that's for sure.
But is there "Ugliness", the lack of beauty?
What is beautiful to someone, is not to someone else.
What is Beauty anyway?

Beauty has become to be measured by external criteria.
It has become a commodity that can be bought & sold.
Beauty has become objectified, like buying a car.
What is Beauty anyway?

This is especially true for women.
Women are objectified & judged on their perceived qualities of beauty.
Qualities that have been created by men for their own personal appetites
What is Beauty anyway?

Beauty has been objectified.
Beauty has been sexualised.
Beauty has been commercilised.
Beauty has been commodified
Beauty has been codified.
Beauty has been formulised.
Beauty has been sanitised
Beauty has been rarified.
Beauty has been externalised.
Beauty has been appropriated.
Beauty has been materialised.
Beauty has been solidified.
Beauty has been miniaturised.
Beauty has been pasteurised.
Beauty has been homogonised.
Beauty has been judgmentalised
Beauty has been LOST.

What is Beauty anyway?

Everyone is beautiful, that is for sure.
Beauty comes from within the person.
Beauty comes from one's heart.
Beauty cannot be bought & sold.
Beauty is not a commodity.
Beauty is a summation of all your values & ideals.
Beauty is who you really are inside when you costume is taken off.
Beauty is the real you, without all the external makeup.
Beauty is you be naked on the inside.
Beauty cannot be faked or manufactured.

So, what is Beauty anyway?

What Is Beauty Anyway?

"The Don"
14.05.2020

The Devil's Child

She was never good at school.
She broke all the rules.
She's tough, street smart & hot as hell.
She's the Devil's Child.

She's a battler, she's struggled all her life.
She has lived many lives, she has so many stories to tell.
If anyone actually stopped & took the time to listen.
She's the Devil's Child.

She's rough & tough, that's true.
She's always being misjudged but isn't that the way of the world?
She's the Wild Child from the Western Suburbs.
She's the Devil's Child.

She's got a heart of gold, loyal & a friend through & through.
She tries to help others even though she claims she has a cold heart.
She's always been the underrated & dismissed by others.
She's the Devil's Child.

She's made her own way in life, against all odds.
She lives life on her own terms & takes no shit from no one.
She never gives up, she's one very stubborn SOB.
She's the Devil's Child.

She's extremely independent, she knows what to do.
Many have dismissed her & written her off.
They really don't know her at all & that really pisses me off.
She's the Devil's Child.

She's beautiful in her wild, crazy ways.
She's as innocent as a child, so free to have fun.
She's a complicated being just like everyone.
She's the Devil's Child.

She will never grow old because she's never grown up.
It's nothing she's interested in, it's not she's about.
I am so glad I met this wonderful spirit.
I am so glad I'm a friend, of The Devil's Child.

"The Don"
16.05.2020

The Faraday Cage

I'm locked up inside my head.
Wishing that I was Dead.
Did you hear what the man said.
You are in The Faraday Cage.

You are overthinking things.
Just allow for what Life brings.
It's not over until the Fat Lady sings.
You are in The Faraday Cage.

Don't complain, it is what it is.
That's the way it is in showbiz.
Life is short but it's one big fiz.
You are living in The Faraday Cage.

Que sera sera, what will be, will be.
The Future's not yours to see.
You pay no rent, you are living for free.
You are thriving in The Faraday Cage.

You're having trouble with your sleep.
Paranoia runs deep.
There's plenty of fear & it's yours to keep.
You are having fun in The Faraday Cage.

The sky & the ground feel like walls.
The air that surrounds you feels like halls.
Do you hear the sound of the wind when it calls?
You are locked in The Faraday Cage.

Life is fun, life is a blast.
Don't try to escape from your past.
You live in the moment but that won't last.
You are a prisoner in The Faraday Cage.

You try to escape, you try to run.
In your hands you're holding a gun.
Listen to "Kurt" when he said, "Life ain't any fun".
You are dying in The Faraday Cage.

You pray to God for help & salvation.
You wait & wait, what's the procrastination.
All you get is more torment & damnation.
You are suffering in The Faraday Cage.

You look to the Devil for a way out of your situation.
She's so hot & sexy with her sassy presentation.
She's got you hooked & it's your damnation.
You are in living in Hell, in The Faraday Cage.

Stop struggling & fighting, just accept your fate.
When Judgement Day comes & you're standing at that Pearly Gate.
Be brave, be strong & accept your fate.
You have lived in The Faraday Cage.

The Faraday Cage

"The Don"
16.05.2020

Infinity
(Ad Infinitum)

It's not the End.
We're on the road again.
I love to travel.
I love adventures.
You are my friend.
Together forever.
What's around the bend?
You can't see round corners.
Or can you?
Will you stay awhile longer?
I've got places to go.
People to see.
Nothing's for free.
Take one, it's free.
Life is short
Death is long.
I think I've overstayed my welcome.
I must go now.
On with the show.
The show must go on.
Break a leg.
That is so mean.
What does that mean anyway?
The band plays its last song.
Time for last drinks.
The bar is closing.
See you around some time.
I'll be back.
Hello old friend.
I never thought I'd see you again?
It's the last Waltz.
The last Waltz lasts forever.

Dance me to the end of Love.
I feel like dancing.
Saturday Night Fever.
You're just Jive Talking.
Whether you're a lover or whether you're a mother.
You're staying alive.
This is the End, my friend, my only friend, The End.
I'm the Midnight Creeper.
I'm the Midnight Rambler.
I'm just a ramblin' man.
I'm Love sick.
I'm sick of love.
Love is a drug.
Happiness is a warm gun.
It's a bad moon rising.
Nowhere man has nothing to lose.
Don't catch my disease.
Where not all in this together.
Love is a battlefield.
So long Marianne, I'm going off with Suzanne.
Suzanne gives good a good blowjob.
But don't go home with a hard-on.
It'll just drive you INSANE.
Insanity is a gift.
God acts in mysterious ways.
Don't even try to predict the unpredictable.
Mountain high, river deep
Let's go down to the river to pray.
Take it to the river, drop it in the water.
The river of chosen dreams.
Down by the river, I killed my baby....dead!
Today, tomorrow & forever.
Forever is a long time.
Tomorrow never comes.
Today will last a lifetime.

Ad Infinitum, so long, goodbye.
Hallelujah, it's the crack of Dawn.
Hello, goodbye, fare thee well.
Sing me a sad song about love gone wrong.
Welcome to The Machine.
Lucy had diamonds in her hair.
I've got diamonds on the soles of my shoes.
Shine on, you crazy diamond.
Wish you were here too.
Everything is beautiful, in its own way.
What's this crazy thing called? Love.
What's this crazy thing called Love?
Lucy had diamonds in her hair.
I've diamonds on the soles of my shoes.
We can be Heroes, forever & ever.
At least for one day.
Come with me?
What d'ya say?

Infinity
(Ad Infinitum)

"The Don"
17.05.2020

Struggle Street

Ain't got enough money to eat.
Struggle Street, Struggle Street.
Can't pay my rent.
Struggle Street, Struggle Street.
I can't buy new clothes.
Struggle Street, Struggle Street.
Ain't got no TV.
Struggle Street, Struggle Street.
Nothing comes for free.
Struggle Street, Struggle Street.
Ain't got no place to live.
Struggle Street, Struggle Street.
Ain't got nothing to give.
Struggle Street, Struggle Street.
My fridge is bare.
Struggle Street, Struggle Street.
Hell, I even got no fridge.
Struggle Street, Struggle Street.
Ain't got no bed.
Struggle Street, Struggle Street.
Did you hear what I said.
Struggle Street, Struggle Street.
Nobody gives a damn.
Struggle Street, Struggle Street.
If you can't pay the man.
Struggle Street, Struggle Street.
I'm all by myself.
Struggle Street, Struggle Street
Sitting on my park bench.
Struggle Street, Struggle Street.
I got holes in my shoes.
Struggle Street, Struggle Street.
I live the Blues.
Struggle Street, Struggle Street.
Don't wash my hair.
Struggle Street, Struggle Street.

My cupboard shelves are bare.
Struggle Street, Struggle Street.
The Life is bad out here.
Struggle Street, Struggle Street.
I'm constantly living in Fear.
Struggle Street, Struggle Street.
Will I be killed in my sleep?
Struggle Street, Struggle Street.
I'm in this way too deep.
Struggle Street, Struggle Street.
Christ, this ain't fair.
Struggle Street, Struggle Street.
People stop & stare.
Struggle Street, Struggle Street.
Is this my fate?
Struggle Street, Struggle Street.
To live forever on....
Struggle Street, Struggle Street.
I'm living on...
Struggle Street, Struggle Street.
That's where we all meet.
Struggle Street, Struggle Street.
Come over & visit.
Struggle Street, Struggle Street.
You don't have to stay long, just a meet & greet.
Down on Struggle Street, Struggle Street.
That's where I'll be.
On Struggle Street, Struggle Street.
I'm living on...
Struggle Street, Struggle Street.
I'm living on...
Struggle Street, Struggle Street.
I'm living on...
Struggle Street, Struggle Street.
Yeah!
Struggle Street, Struggle Street.

Did you hear me?
Down on Struggle Street, Struggle Street.
You ain't listening!
Struggle Street, Struggle Street.
Listen to me!
Struggle Street, Struggle Street.
I'm living on...
Struggle Street, Struggle Street.
Yeah!
Struggle Street, Struggle Street.
I'm living on...
Struggle Street, Struggle Street.
What I'd say?
Struggle Street, Struggle Street
I'm living on...
Struggle Street, Struggle Street.

Number 666, Struggle Street.
Struggle Street, Struggle Street.

Struggle Street, Struggle Street.
It's the place to meet.

Struggle Street

"The Don"
17.05.2020

The Polemicist

He's controversial.
He's argumentative.
He's adversarial.
He's an agitator.
He's oppositional.
He's can Agent Provacateur.
He's a non-conformist.
He's enigmatic.
He's mysterious.
He's got no face.
He's got no nation.
He's an "international man of mystery".
He's a trouble-maker.
He's an anarchist.
He's a writer.
He's a poet.
He's a Lo♥er.
He's a Sinner.
He's a "shit-stirrer".
He's "The Polemicist".

"The Don"
18.05.2020.

The Merman

Fuck that booby, "Aquaman".
Fuck that nobody, "Poseidon".
Fuck that idiot, "The Sub-Mariner".
There is only one superhero that rules the sea.
The Merman!

He swims like a dolphin.
He bites like a shark.
He's majestic like a whale.
He glides like a stingray.
He's, The Merman.

His tongue is his lethal weapon.
He can use like an arrow.
It can be launched from his mouth with deadly force.
It is extremely accurate.
He's, The Merman.

He never misses his target.
He then reels it back in.
Like a fishing rod with its prey on the end.
You are a gonna, if you are on the end of his tongue.
He's, The Merman.

His tongue is a powerful thing.
But he can use it for good as well.
He'll use to make Lo♥e to all the other Mermaids of the sea.
He's also a Lo♥er.
He's, The Merman, King of the Sea.

He'll start real slow.
Licking her scaly body.
Then, he'll concentrate on that special place at the top of her fin.
Just where her legs meet if she was a human.
He likes to lick & stick right in.
He's, The Merman, Lo♥er of the Sea.

He'll make his beautiful Mermaid moan & cry with delight.
The way he uses his tongue to penetrate & get to all the hidden places.
"Don't stop! Don't stop!"
She screams through the bubbles of water.
He'll make her come like never before.
Cause, he's, The Merman, King of the Sea.

The Merman

"The Don"
18.05.2020

Let's Get High

I wanna get you high.
I wanna make you free.
I wanna see you be a free spirit.
I wanna make you feel.
I wanna give you pleasure.
I wanna set you on fire.
Come on, Let's Get High.

I wanna see you get high
I wanna see you be free.
I wanna see your spirit fly off into the sky
I wanna see you feel.
I see you in pleasure.
I wanna see you on fire.
Come on, Let's Get Higher.

Are you scared to get high?
Are you scared to be free?
Are you scared to let your spirit fly off into the sky?
Are you scared to feel?
Are you scared to be on fire?
Come on, Let's Get Higher & Higher.

Don't be scared to get high.
Don't be scared to be free.
Don't be scared to let your spirit fly off into the sky.
Don't be scared to feel.
Don't be scared to be on fire.
Come on, Let's Get Higher, Higher & Higher.

I'll be you when you get high.
I'll be you when you become free.
I'll be you when you let your spirit fly off into the sky.
I'll be you when you start to feel.
I'll be you when you when you set yourself on fire.
Come on, together, Let's Get Higher, Higher, Higher & Higher.

"The Don"
18.05.2020

Troubled Mind

I've got crazy dreams.
I'd committed a crime.
The cops were interrogating me.
Should I admit my guilt.
I've got a Troubled Mind.

The interview was open to the public.
People filed in to the room be witnesses.
There were faces I recognised in the crowd.
It seemed like it was a very popular event.
I must have a Troubled Mind.

I saw my mother & brother sitting together.
I saw my cousins watching me intently.
Should I admit my guilt here & now.
I started to cry for my indiscretion.
It seems I've got a Troubled Mind.

Even the cops were strange.
They were a family, father, mother & a daughter.
They were dressed in normal street clothes.
They used strange interview techniques.
Yes, I've got a Troubled Mind.

The male cop used mind games on me.
He made me stretch out my hand.
He then got a knife said he would cut off two fingers.
I must admit my guilt or else, two fingers were gone.
OMG, do I have a Troubled Mind.

He said it won't hurt if I tell him the truth.
The people gave out a gasp of fear.
I looked at my mother, brother & cousin.
I could see in their faces the crime I had done.
WTF, I've got a Troubled Mind.

I closed my eyes as he started to cut.
I tried to remember what I had heard of muscle memory.
Of soldiers in in war that had lost a limb but could still feel it.
They could still feel it long after it was gone.
Boy oh boy, do I have a Troubled Mind.

I imagined my hand with all of its fingers intact.
I heard the sound of the knife cutting through flesh & bone.
I was strong, I kept my mind focused.
I didn't feel any pain as two fingers were removed.
Man alive, I've got a Troubled Mind.

I opened my eyes to see the result.
I clenched my hand into a fist to see if it was alright.
My fingers were still there, it was all a bad dream.
It must be all because I've got a Troubled Mind.

Troubled Mind

"The Don"
19.05.2020

Children of the Revolution

The planet is being fucked.
By politicians who just wanna make a buck.
They are not interested in saving our home.
We have to accept that we have to go it alone.
So, come on & let's do it, there's no time for confusion.
Because we are the Children of the Revolution

Global warming is accelerating at an ever increasing pace.
It could mean the extinction of the whole Human Race.
The Polar ice is melting more & more each year, reaching our shore.
The water is getting higher it's knocking at our door.
The planet is chocking with all the pollution.
Time to awaken the Children of the Revolution.

Planet Earth is choking on the human-made stench.
We can no longer just fuck around & sit an s bench.
Multinational companies must be held accountable for what they've done.
They hold Humanity hostage at the end of a gun.
Young people protest because that know what's the solution.
It's time for the Children of the Revolution.

It's time to take action, to take things into our hands.
People must join together, protest & make our demands.
We must take it to the streets, stop the traffic with our numbers & gear.
That's the only way politicians will listen & tremble with fear.
That's the only time they will act, when the fear their own abolition.
We are here & we are the Children of the Revolution.

We're gonna scream & shout.
Gonna let it all hang out.
We'll protest every day & every night.
You won't get us out of your sight
We gonna create massive confusion.
Because we're the Children of the Revolution.

No, you won't fool the children of the revolution.
No, you won't fool the children of the revolution.
No, no, no way!

No, you won't fool the children of the revolution.
No, you won't fool the children of the revolution.
Hear what I say!
No, no, way!

Children of the Revolution

"The Don"
19.05.2020

True Lo♥e

I'm looking for Mr Right.
I'm looking for my ideal mate.
I'm looking for the one who'll set my heart on fire.
I'm looking for my soul mate.
I'm looking for True Lo♥e.

I'm looking for my Hippie Chick.
I'm looking for my honey on a stick.
I'm looking for my wild child.
I'm looking for the one that's gonna make me Lo♥e sick.
I'm looking for my True Lo♥e.

I'm looking for a Lo♥e that lasts forever.
I'm looking for the one that strokes my beaver.
I'm looking for the one that makes my skin go tingle.
I'm looking for the one that will be my single.
Where can I find my True Lo♥e?

I keep on searching but I'm always let down.
There must be more to this than going round & around?
I'm always let down by what there's about.
It just makes me want to jump & shoot.
Where is my True Lo♥e?

I come to the conclusion.
To clarify all this confusion.
The is no right person, it's just a delusion.
This is the answer, this the solution.
There is s no True Lo♥e!

Live in the moment & just Lo♥e the one you're with.
That's all you can do, that's all you can give.
Stop searching for that Ideal mate.
Open the door to others, open the gate.
Because there is no such thing as True Lo♥e.

"The Don"
19.05.2020

Red Left Hand
(Mano Sinistra Rossa)

I'm the Devil's Child.
I'm the Sinner Man.
I sit on the left hand of The Father.
I've got a Red Left Hand.

I like to sin.
I like to breathe fire.
I will make you a Sinner.
I've got a Red Left Hand.

I will tempt you with pleasure.
I will tempt you with desire.
I will make you promises I have no intention to keep.
I've got a Red Left Hand.

I will shower you with words.
I will dazzle you with lights.
I will promise you all manner of delights.
I've got a Red Left Hand.

You can't escape my power.
You can't run & hide.
I am omnipotent.
I've got a Red Left Hand.

My eyes a red as the blood in your veins.
My breath is hotter than the sun.
My skin is white & as cold as ice.
I've got a Red Left Hand.

I live in the depths of your soul.
I live in the bowels of your being.
I live in in a place everyone knows as Hell.
I am the one with the Red Left Hand.

Be afraid, very afraid of me.
I will tell that I can set your soul free.
But there is a heavy price that you must pay.
Because you're making a deal with the Red Left Hand.

Don't try to negotiate, it will be no use.
Once the deal is done, it is sealed with your blood.
Don't expect to walk away when the dancing is done.
You have sold your soul to the one with the Red Left Hand.

Red Left Hand

"The Don"
19.05.2020

Dr Love

(The Lo♥e Doctor)

Are you looking for Love?
You've come to the right place.
Are you looking for fun?
Well, then I'm your guy.
Are you looking for a good for a good time?
Don't look any further.
You've found the right guy.
Cause I'm Dr Lo♥e.
The Lo♥e Doctor.

I know what do to make you happy.
I know what to do to take you high.
I know what to do to rock you boat.
I know what to do ignite your fire.
I know what to do to make you explode with passion.
I know what to do to reignite your Desire.
You've found the right guy.
Cause I'm Dr Lo♥e.
The Lo♥e Doctor.

You'd lost your Libido.
You'd lost your Desire.
You'd lost you confidence.
You'd lost your Fire.
You'd lost your Heart.
You'd lost you Sex.
You've found the right guy.
Cause I'm Dr Lo♥e.
The Lo♥e Doctor.

I know what to do.
I know what to say.
I know how to make you feel.
I know how to see you, like you want to be seen.
I know how unlock your Heart.
I know the path to the Tunnel of Lo♥e.
You've found the right guy.
Cause I'm Dr Lo♥e.
The Lo♥e Doctor.

You've been used & abused.
You've been taken for a ride.
You've been mistreated.
You've been told you're no good.
You've been told you're too old.
You've lost you power.
You've found the right guy.
Cause I'm Dr Lo♥e.
The Lo♥e Doctor.

You've lost your way.
You've forgotten what to say.
You've had a bad time.
You've been led astray.
You've been sad & lonely for such a long time.
You've been doubting & second guessing yourself.
But you've found the right guy.
Cause I'm Dr Lo♥e.
The Lo♥e Doctor.

Don't look any more.
Don't run & hide.
Don't need to pretend that you're happy inside.
Don't shy away.
Don't be as cold as ice.
Don't keep your door closed.
Cause, you've found the right guy.
Cause I'm Dr Lo♥e.
The Lo♥e Doctor.

He'll teach you to Lo♥e yourself again.
He'll give good medicine.
He'll make you powerful again.
He'll unlock the Feminine.
He'll make you the boss.
He'll give you the Power.
You've found the right guy.
Cause he's Dr Lo♥e.
The Lo♥e Doctor.

You can scream & shout.
You can let it all hang out.
You can raise your hands in the air.
You can shout & swear.
You can fuck as much as you like.
You can stay high forever
Cause, you've found the right guy.
Cause I'm Dr Lo❤e.
The Lo❤e Doctor.

"Doctor, Doctor, give me the news,
I've got a bad case of loving you.
No pills gonna cure my ills."

You've found the right guy.
You've found the right place.
I'm open 24/7.
365 days in year.
I never close.
My doors are always open.
You don't need to make a booking.
Just walk right.
There's no waiting time.
There's no waiting room.
I take nice easy.
I've got a slow hand.
I don't need to rush
I've got all the time in the world
We're not going anywhere.
This is our world.
Satisfaction guaranteed.
You'll be coming for more.
I never refuse.
I'll never let you down.
You've found the right guy.
Cause I'm Dr Lo❤e.
The Lo❤e Doctor.

That's right, you've found the right guy.
Cause I'm Dr Lo♥e.
The Lo♥e Doctor.

I'll treat you right, you've found the right guy.
Cause I'm Dr Lo♥e.
The Lo♥e Doctor.

I have ancient knowledge from The East.
You've found the right guy.
Cause I'm Dr Lo♥e.
The Lo♥e Doctor.

Dr Love

(The Lo♥e Doctor)

"The Don"
18.05.2020

Mindmap

Where are we going?
What is our destination?
Will we get there soon?
Are there any bends on this rocky road?
I can't see very far ahead.
It's very foggy.
Are you enjoying the ride?
Are we there yet?
Can we stop for a rest?
It's a long way to go.
The scenery is very nice.
Although sometimes it's a bit scary.
I can't see too far ahead.
I think I am lost.
Can you tell me where we're going?
Is it a nice place?
Is it some sort of resort?
I think I need a rest!
I can't keep up this pace.
We're moving way too fast.
Can't we slow down?
We are already late.
This is a very important date.
We can't waste time.
We've been travelling a long way.
There's still a long way to go.
I'm getting very tired.
We're making good time.
We'll be there very soon.

The road is very windy.
It's a long windy road.
Can we have some music?
Some music for the road.
It will ease my boredom.
Maybe some AC/DC or Deep Purple?
Can we play it real loud?
To block out the noise.
We're very close now.
Put the foot on the gas.
Let this baby rip.
Let's go Space Truckin'.
This is a driving machine.
It has power to burn.
I think it's the Batmobile.
It's a beautiful ride.
You've been a really good friend.
Great to ride with you.
You're a great conversationalist.
You've got so many good stories to tell.
We should do this again sometime.
Well, this is the end, my friend.
I've had a good time.
Maybe, I'll see you again.
We're going in different directions.
Our paths might cross again, sometime.

"The Don"
20.05.2020

Lo♥e You

Lo♥e the way you talk.
Lo♥e the way you think.
Lo♥e the way you feel.
Lo♥e the way you act.
Lo♥e the way you walk.
Lo♥e the way you look.
Lo♥e the way you smile.
Lo♥e the way you laugh.
Lo♥e the way you care.
Lo♥e the way you are so kind.
Lo♥e the way you make me feel.
Lo♥e the way you work so hard.
Lo♥e the way you stay so positive.
Lo♥e the way you are so intelligent.
Lo♥e the way you are so focused.
Lo♥e the way you never complain.
Lo♥e the way you never give up.
Lo♥e the way you are so determined.
Lo♥e the way you walk through your pain.
Lo♥e the way you make Lo♥e.
Lo♥e the way you make me Lo♥e.
Lo♥e the way you Lo♥e.

"The Don"
21.05.2020

Stress

Stress is in my head.
Stress is in my mind.
Stress is noise.
Stress not let you sleep.
Stress causes cancer.
Stress will make you blind.
Stress will make you crazy.
Stress will drive you insane.
Stress will destroy your life.
Stress will fuck you up big time.
Stress will fuck with your thoughts.
Stress will fuck with your feelings.
Stress will make you do & say crazy shit.
Stress will take you down into the abyss.
Stress will send you into a black hole of despair.
Stress will send you psycho.
Stress will make you see crazy things.
Stress will play with your desires.
Stress will make you take chances.
Stress will make you test you luck.
Stress will play havoc when you fuck.
Stress will destroy your mind!
Stress will send you into outta Space & maybe never return.
Stress will not pay your mortgage, your bills or your phone.
Stress will make you lose all your friends.
Stress will keep back again & again.
Stress will enchain you fear & misery.
Stress will tear you apart from ear to ear.

Stress will take that smile off your face.
Stress will let you join the rest of the Human Race.
Stress will put a frown on your dial.
Stress will let you drown in a quagmire.
Stress will make you eat your excrement.
Stress will never stop, it is very incessant.
Stress will take you down a narrow path of suffering & pain.
Stress will attack your thoughts & drive you mad & insane.
Stress will make you shit yourself & give you panic attacks.
Stress will not give up & keep on doing it, again & again.
Stress will give you a shovel & make you dig your own grave.
Stress will make you lie down in it & make you pray to God or the Devil, whichever you worship.
Stress will make you cry & shout for it to stop.
Stress will make you cry for your Death to come quickly, for it to be the End.
Stress will kill you & you'll never rise again from your ashes, & that'll be your end, my friend.

Stress

"The Don"
21.05.2020

Part Time Lo♥er

I need a part time Lo♥er.
One who doesn't hang around.

I need a part time Lo♥er.
One who doesn't need full time loving.

I need a part time Lo♥er.
One who doesn't need need to stay.

I need a part time Lo♥er.
One who just wants to play.

I need a part time Lo♥er.
One who just wants to fuck.

I need a part time Lo♥er.
One who doesn't need stay around.

I need a part time Lo♥er.
One who doesn't want to hang on.

I need a part time Lo♥er.
One who won't drive me crazy.

I need a part time Lo♥er.
One who lives her own life.

I need a part time Lo♥er.
One who doesn't need to be my wife.

I need a part time Lo♥er.
One who doesn't need see me all the time.

I need a part time Lo♥er.
One who doesn't need me hanging round.

I need a part time Lo♥er.
One who doesn't need eating her food.

I need a part time Lo♥er.
One who just needs me for a fuck.

I need a part time Lo♥er.
One who doesn't need stay around.

I need a part time Lo♥er.
One who doesn't want to hang on.

I need a part time Lo♥er.
One who won't drive me crazy.

I need a part time Lo♥er.
One who lives her own life.

I need a part time Lo♥er.
One who doesn't need to be my wife.

I need a part time Lo♥er.
One who doesn't need see me all the time.

I need a part time Lo♥er.
One who doesn't need me hanging round.

I need a part time Lo♥er.
One who doesn't need me eating her food.

I need a part time Lo♥er.
One who just needs me & then just says see ya later.

I need a part time Lo♥er.
One who doesn't need me to drive her around.

I need a part time Lo♥er.
One who has her own fun.

I need a part time Lo♥er.
One who music & love in her heart.

I need a part time Lo♥er.
One who is creative & kind at heart.

I need a part time Lo♥er.
One who doesn't need to be prim & proper.

I need a part time Lo♥er.
One who is a free spirit & has a free soul.

I need a part time Lo❤er.
One who likes to smoke marijuana & get high.

I need a part time Lo❤er.
One who doesn't need a lavish lifestyle.

I need a part time Lo❤er.
One who doesn't always need to look her best.

I need a part time Lo❤er.
One who doesn't want to be like all the rest.

I need a part time Lo❤er.
One who likes to have her freedom.

I need a part time Lo❤er.
One who values & likes her independence.

I need a part time Lo❤er.
One who doesn't want to move in.

I need a part time Lo❤er.
One who doesn't need to see me all the time.

I need a part time Lo❤er.
One who doesn't need constant reassurance about how beautiful she is.

I need a part time Lo❤er.
One who has a monobrow.

I need a part time Lo❤er.
One who has hair in her armpits.

I need a part time Lo❤er.
One who's name is Frida Khalo.

"The Don"
21.05.2020

Validation
(I Don't Need No)

I don't need your approval.
I don't need you to like me.
I don't seek your Love.
I don't require you ok.
I don't seek that you like me.
I don't require your opinion.
I don't care if you like me or not.
I can live without your participation.
I don't need your Validation.

I don't seek your attention.
I don't require your consideration.
I don't live for your sympathy.
I don't require your support.
I don't need your criticism.
I don't seek your corroboration
I can live securely in myself.
I don't require your interpretation.
I don't require your Validation.

I don't need you to feed my ego.
I don't require you drool over me.
I don't seek your authorisation.
I don't require your consent.
I don't need your admiration.
I don't seek your acceptance.
I can live comfortably with my own self-image.
I don't look for your affirmation.
I don't seek your Validation.

"The Don"
21.05.2020

The Music Goes Round My Head

There is music inside my brain.
There is music inside my soul.
There is music inside my body.
There is music inside my heart.
There is music inside my mind.
There is music inside my eyes.
There is music inside my face.
There is music inside my mouth.
There is music inside my arms.
There is music inside my hands.
There is music inside my legs.
There is music inside my feet.
There is music inside my cells.
There is music inside my DNA.

And the music goes round my head.
The music won't stop until I'm dead.
Yes, the music goes round my head.
Even when I'm sleeping in my bed.
Yes, the music goes round my head.

There is Reo Speedwagon.
There is Deep Purple.
There is Patti Smith.
There is The Doors.
There is The Rolling Sones.
There is Neil Young.
There is Leonard Cohen.
There is Gerry & the Pacemakers.
There is The Stray Cats.
There is The Angels.
There is Van Morrison.

There is Nirvana.
There is Tom Jones.
There is Skyhooks.
There is Dire Straits.
There is Cream.
There is The Beatles.
There is Donovan.
There is Iron Butterfly.
There is Elvis Presley.
There is Shirley Bassey.
There is The Moody Blues.
There is Pink Floyd.
There is Jimi Hendrix.
There is AC/DC.
There is Chuck Berry.
There is The Monkeys.
There is Melanie.
There is Led Zeppelin.
There is Marianne Faithful.
There is Eric Clapton.
There is Arlo Guthrie.
There is The Stranglers.
Buddy Holly & The Crickets.
There is The Sex Pistols.
There is David Bowie.
There is the Archies.
There is Nancy Sinatra.
There is Robert Palmer.
There is Toto.
There is Dean Martin.
There is Joan Baez.
There is Perry Como.
There is Roberta Flack.

There is Tony Joe White.
There Harry Manx.
Lou Reed.
Bill Haley & The Comets.
There is Don McLean.
There is Nina Simone.
There is Elton John.
There is Queen.
There is Cat Stevens.
There is Blondie.
There is The Talking Heads.
There is Bob Dylan.
There is more & more & more.

And the music goes round my head.
It will never stop until I'm dead.
Yes, it keeps playing inside my head.
And it won't stop until I'm dead.
Oh, the music keeps on playing inside my head.

In a world full of suffering & pain.
I will keep on singing again & again & again.
And it's keeping me from going insane!

And the Music Goes Round My Head

"The Don"
22.05.2020

Rider from the Storm

There's a hurricane a'blowin' out there.
The wind is a fierce creature.
The rain is like bullets of ice hitting your face.
But your mission is clear.
Nothing is going to get into your way.
There is still a long way to go.
Many more hours to go before you get to your destination.
There will be no rest for you tonight.
You are the rider from the storm.

The wind is talking to you as you surge forward.
It's more of a scream rather than a simple warning.
But you decide not to hear, you reject its foreboding.
The rain on your face feel like the tears falling from your eyes.
It makes the road appear misty & foggy as though you are in a dream.
Bit you are relentless, there is no deviation from your journey.
To seek redemption, a forgiveness, for the things that you've done.
You've been cruel, mean & unkind to many people throughout my life.
You are the rider from the storm.

The wind is so cold it's biting you face.
You nose is frozen solid & it could easily fall off.
Your hands are in the pockets of an old war coat that you're wearing.
You have a beanie on your head is completely soaked through.
Your toes are frozen in your wet socks, in your sodden boots on your feet.
You're drenched to your bones, your muscles shiver & tremble.
But there is no fear in your body, your mind is completely clear.
Your determination does not waver an inch.
You are like an arrow heading straight to the centre.
You are the rider from the storm.

What will you do when you arrive at your destination?
What will you say to the keeper of the gate to let you go through?
Will you tell her a story about how it was never your fault.
How it was bad luck, you were a victim of circumstances.
That you were in the wrong place at the wrong time.
How others misunderstood you & your intentions.
That you never intended it to happen.
It got outta hand, you lost control.
That your mind went blank & forgot where you were.
That mind exploded with confusion & delusion about the situation.
How it was all about love, honour & pride.

Or,

Will you tell the truth?
Of how you are weak, full of guilt & crippled inside.
And that you are, the rider from the storm!

Rider from the Storm

"The Don"
22.05.2020

The Doors of Perception

What can you see through your eyes?
Can you see through walls?
Can you see through to your soul?
Can you see where you came from?
Can you see where you are going?
Can you see round corners?
Can you see round the bend?
Can you see the Future?
Can you see what tomorrow will bring?
Can you see into my head?
Can you see into my mind?
Can you see into my heart?
Can you see who I am?
Can you see your direction?
Can you see where you're going?
Can you see where you've been?
Can you see the light at the end of the tunnel?
Can you see your creation?
Can you see your own Death!

"The Don"
22.05.2020

The Lunatics Are in My Head

I hear voices inside my head.
They are talking to me but I don't understand what the words mean.
The voices have no obvious pattern, structure or meaning that I can make any sense of.
Is it just gibberish & nonsense?
Maybe, there is a meaning to all of this.
The Lunatics are in my head.

There is lots of confusion inside my head.
I have a lot of noise inside my brain
There is static distortion inside my head.
My mind is tuning into mush.
I am losing my mind.
The Lunatics are in my head.

I am becoming mindless.
I am going insane.
It never stops.
They invade my dreams when I'm asleep.
When I'm awake they make me dream.
The Lunatics are in my head.

They are incessant, 24/7.
They never take a break.
They never go on a holiday.
I have tried to knock them out with drugs.
But it's just like food, it only makes them stronger.
The Lunatics are in my head.

I have lost the game.
I have lost control.
They have won the battle.
They have won the war.
They have taken over my mind.
The Lunatics are in my head.

Now, I'm a vegetable.
A shell of a man.
I go to work 5 days a week & don't complain
I have a nice house, a wife & two kids
Make lots of money & drive a nice car.
I am happy now because the Lunatics are in my head.

The Lunatics Are in My Head

"The Don"
22.05.2020

Ketosis

I have neurosis.
I have problems.
I am overweight.
Some might even say obese.
I need to look sexy.
I need to be slim.
I need to lose weight.
I need to be in Ketosis.

I weigh 106 kilos.
I am 61 years young.
I'm 1.8 metres tall.
I'm a son of a gun.
I walk with a swagger.
I stand tall & upright.
I bend for no one.
Except of course, for Ketosis.

My friend Zac laid out on the line.
He didn't mince words, he told it to me straight.
Mate, you look like an old man.
No girl will ever look at you, you're not a good looking man.
You don't look desirable, you don't look attractive.
Get rid of the beard & cut off your hair.
Just by doing these two little things you'll look ten years younger.
That's right my friend, you need to be in Ketosis.

I heard his words, they made sense to me.
It's a world of perception, how you look is why people see.
They can't see what's deep in your heart.
They don't know what's in your soul.
All they can see what's on the outside.
They don't have time to go with for a ride.
Their judgment is quick, are you sexy or not?
The only thing they can see is if you are in Ketosis.

It's not their fault that people are this way.
That judgments are made on looks & perception.
Take some time to make yourself attractive, Zac said to me.
It'll make a huge difference in our vain society.
It is true, beauty is measured by external factors.
There is no point complaining about it, it's a fact know of life.
If you ever want another girl to look at you & get excited?
Then, my friend, you have to be in Ketosis.

So, now I'm on a diet of celery & carrots.
I've cut out carbs & sugars, no pasta or bread.
It's a battle to lose weight & become thin.
Apparently, I have to lose 35 kilos.
To get my desired weight of 85 kilos.
I must be strong & focused if I ever want a fuck again.
"Mind over Matter", that's what drives me forward, that's what is my strength.
That is the way to reach the Nirvana of Ketosis.

Ketosis

"The Don"
23.05.2020

Poem for Bob

His given name is *Robert Zimmerman* but changed it to *Bob Dylan* in 1961.
Some say he got it from *Dylan Thomas*, the Irish poet who he liked, but no one really knows for sure.
He walked into the New York folk scene & blew it away.
No one had ever heard some like him before, said *Paul Stookey*, when he first saw him sing & play.
It was at the *"Gaslight Café"* in Greenwich Village late one November night in 1961.
A night that would change the world of folk music & music generally, forever.

He sat alone in a darkened, on a chair with just his guitar & harmonica slung around his neck.
He was an unassuming, scrawny, young lad with a cap on his head.
He was nothing unusual, nothing special, yet!
It was when he started to sing, with a nasally drawl, like a wannabe Woody Guthrie, that started to listen.
What the fuck was coming out of his mouth, what the fuck was he singing.
It wasn't a song that anyone had heard before, of lost love or ships washed up on a shore.

It was a song about what had happened that day.
Of an incident that was just in the news, it was in all the papers.
His song was a *"talking song"* about this story, it was mesmerising, hypnotic & alluring.
It went on for seventeen minutes or longer but it only seemed like a few seconds where was I frozen in my chair.
My mind was blown out, I was shivering in delight.
I had had just been a witness to a momentous event.
The world had just changed forever that moment.

That song was called *"Talking Bear Mountain Picnic Massacre Blues"*.
Listen to it, if you've ever got the time.

Bob is an enigma, a mystery no one can fathom.
That's one of the reasons why I like him.
He generally does his own thing, goes by his own rules & plays his own tune.
He keeps on touring on his *"Never Ending Tour"* & probably die on stage one night.
He never plays a song the same way again.
Each time it's a new arrangement, a new interpretation, to give it new life.
He's written thousands of songs throughout his life.

He's sheltered me from the storms & the idiot winds that have blown.
Of when I was tangled up in blue & all along the watchtower.
He was there when I lost my dignity & asked Mr Tambourine Man to play a song for me.
I was blowin' in the wind out on Highway 61.
Where I was living like a rolling stone.
That's where I was asked by God to kill him a son.
I knew what to say, "where does it have to be done?"
I've been to the gates of Eden & I've the hard rain falling.
I've served everybody on that slow train coming.
But I can't forget when I cried for Ophelia on Desolation Row & when I shouted, "It's alright ma, I'm only bleeding"!

Bob Dylan (Robert Zimmerman)
Born: 24th May, 1941
Duluth, Minnesota.

"The Don"
23.05.2020

I am a Product

I am a product.
I am a commodity.
I can be bought & sold for a very small fee.
Just a few dollars, is all I need.
I'm not greedy, I just need some food to eat & a bed to sleep in.

I'm on the shelf now.
My "used by" date has expired.
I'm gathering dust like those unwanted CDs & DVDs of yesteryear, such a long time ago.
I am an antique, a curiosity, some might even say a dinosaur.
My time has long gone, I'm no longer a desirable commodity in the marketplace.

I must rebrand myself, make myself desirable once again.
Repackage my appearance & make look young & appealing.
Pretty soon I'll a top selling product, flying out through those doors.
There will be a que to buy & sell me like they did before.
I will be wanted, needed & played with once more.
I am writing the story, I'm creating a myth of myself.
It's all just fiction but no one will ever be able to guess.

The story is a good one & that's for sure.
It's how I was left & found in front of a church door.
Of how I was an orphan, unwanted & unloved.
Brought up in a monastery where I was taught how to Love.
I was taught to be strong & faith in myself.
That no matter your beginnings, you decide your own fate

I struggled all of my life to be a poet, to set people free.
Through my words I wanted to make people feel.
All of the things that I felt & that were deep inside me.
It doesn't matter that you have no education.
You have a life & that's the only requirement.
Just speak what you feel & create your own story.

One to be bought & sold throughout the whole Universe for an ETERNITY.

"The Don"
23.05.2020

Danger Man

Danger Man is full of trouble.
Danger Man doesn't play by the rules.
Danger Man plays with fire.
Danger Man goes where no one else dares.
Danger Man likes to take risks.
Danger Man has no fear.
Danger Man likes adventure.
Danger Man puts his life on the line.
Danger Man goes where no one else goes.
Danger Man does what no one else does.
Danger Man is a solitary man.
Danger Man lives a solitary life.
Danger Man is a lonely man.
Danger Man lives a lonely life.
Danger Man, he causes problems.
Danger Man, he likes to burn.
Danger Man is too hot to touch.
Danger Man doesn't form any attachments.
Danger Man loves & leaves you.
Danger Man may never return.
Danger Man does what no other man can.
Danger Man is a trouble-maker.
Danger Man lives a life of danger.
Danger Man is a dangerous man.

Don't get involved with the Danger Man.
BE SCARED of the Danger Man.
TAKE care of the Danger Man.
BEWARE of the Danger Man.
RUN away from the Danger Man.
LOOK out for the Danger Man.

LOOK OUT, LOOK OUT, Danger Man about!

"The Don"
24.05.2020

You're No Good

I've been told it all my life.
You're a failure.
You are stupid.
You are lazy.
You'll never end up to anything.
You're No Good!

You're not good at school.
You break all the rules.
You need to conform.
You need to do what you're told.
You need lick my arse.
Because You're No Good.

You have no imagination.
You have no creativity.
You can't spell or write.
You bring bad luck.
Hell, you can't even speak properly.
Baby, You're No Good.

You're a failure.
You're a loser.
You have no friends.
Nobody even likes you.
Don't even bother to try.
Because, baby You're No Good.

You've been told this your whole life.
You've been put down.
You've been abused.
You've been ridiculed.
You've been laughed at.
That, You're No Good.

But you've had enough of this shit.
It's time to take back control of your life.
It's time to play by your own rules.
It's time to play the "Game of Life" your own way.
It's time not to listen to what others say.
That, You're No Good.

It's time to take back your power.
It's time to regain your strength.
It's time to reclaim your identity.
It's time to say, "FUCK YOU ALL"!
"I don't need you!
I can do it all by myself!"
It's time to break the chains,
To that world that told you,
That, You're No Good!

You're No Good

"The Don"
24.05.2020

Restless Mind

I can't shut down my mind.
It goes very fast.
It travels at the speed of light.
That's very fast.
I overthink all the time.
I have a Restless Mind.

I must quieten my mind.
It's driving me crazy.
It never stops.
It never has a rest.
It's always switched on.
I have a Restless Mind.

My mind has a mind of its own.
It cannot be controlled.
It is a force of Nature.
It is a powerful force.
It cannot be stopped.
I have a Restless Mind.

It travels the Universe.
Searching for answers.
To the great unknowns.
Why are we here?
What is our purpose?
I have a Restless Mind.

It doesn't stop at just one universe.
It searches all the Multiverses too.
It seems to have no limits.
At the things it can do.
It has no boundaries.
I have a Restless Mind.

It has a vast imagination.
It straddles the vastness of Space.
It has no fears.
It goes wherever it likes.
It does ever it wants.
I have a Restless Mind.

I wish I could control it.
Tell it what to do.
Have some input into it.
So, we could be friends.
Maybe, have a joint mission of discovery.
I have a Restless Mind.

But it won't be tamed.
It is as wild as the sea.
It is as powerful as the wind.
It needs to be free.
Free to roam expanse of Space-Time.
I have a Restless Mind.

I now go to sleep.
But my mind never rests.
My mind never sleeps, like I do.
It doesn't need to.
It is an alien form.
I have a Restless Mind.

It doesn't belong in the material world.
It cannot be explained.
Is it from the spiritual realm?
Is it a form energy?
Or is something completely different?
I have a Restless Mind.

My Restless Mind makes me who I am.
It challenges me all the time.
It keeps me moving along the road of curiosity.
It keeps me exploring the great unknowns.
It never makes me give up.
I love, my Restless Mind.

"The Don"
25.05.2020

Anger
(I'm Angry)

I've been forgotten.
I've been overlooked.
I've been mistreated.
I've been stepped upon.
I've been used.
I've been abused.
I've been rejected.
I've been ejected.
I've been spat on.
I've been shat on.
I've been unloved.
I've been laughed at.
I've been ridiculed.
I've been called ridiculous.
I've been called a loser.
I've been called crazy.
I've been called weird.
I've been called a train wreck, about to happen.
I've been called ugly.
I've been called fatso.
I've been called an old fart.
I've been called lazy.
I've been told I get what I deserve.
I've been called a lost cause.
I've been called desperate.
I've called a "has-been".
I am an angry young ALIEN!

"The Don"
25.05.2020

Everybody Lies

Everybody lies.
No one tells the truth.
If someone tells you that they don't lie.
Well, you know that's not the truth.
That's a lie!
Because Everybody Lies.

Everybody spins a yarn.
Everybody tells a story.
Everybody wants to embellish reality.
Because reality is very boring.
No one is as good as they say.
Because Everybody Lies.

Politicians lie all the time.
They've made it their stock & trade.
We'd actually be surprised if they ever told the truth.
In fact, we'd think it was I lie.
We wouldn't believe them.
Because Everybody Lies.

Teachers tell lies all the time.
They tell you that you must learn this.
It will be important for your future.
Every student knows that this is a lie.
They just have to look at their parents to tell you this.
Everybody Lies.

Parents lie all the time.
To keep you in check.
They promise you this, they promise yet that.
Just so that you do what they say & don't cause trouble.
It's called bribery & we do it all the time.
Because to get what we want, everybody has to Lie.

Even a "White Lie" is lie.
That's just the way it is.
A lie is a lie, is a lie & there is no denying.
There is no escaping it.
That is the TRUTH, Everybody Lies.

"The Don"
25.05.2020

Lost Soul

I'm a lost baby.
I'm a lost child.
I'm a lost being.
I'm a lost mind.
I'm a lost Soul looking for a home.

I've got nowhere to go.
I've got no place to stay.
I've got nowhere to rest.
I've got nowhere to lay.
I'm a lost Soul looking a place for my weary bones.

Nobody wants me.
Nobody needs me.
Nobody loves me.
I'm all alone
I'm a lost Soul looking for a port.

Can someone help me?
Just for a night?
I won't be any trouble.
I'll be very quiet.
I'm a lost Soul looking for a bed.

I won't make a mess.
I don't even snore.
I'll just have a quick rest.
Then I'll be out through your door.
I'm a lost Soul looking for a heart.

You can stay at my place.
There's always room for one more.
Make yourself at home.
Treat it like your own.
You're a Lost Soul & you've just found a home.

It's the home for Lost Souls.

"The Don"
25.05.2020

Welcome to The Machine

You must be productive.
You must be efficient.
You must be focused.
You must be reliable.
You must be fast.
You must be precise.
You must be a Machine.

Don't stop.
Don't look around.
Don't talk to anyone.
Don't think.
Don't feel.
Don't go to sleep.
You must be a Machine.

You must be punctual.
You must be careful.
You must be skilful.
You must be accurate.
You must be coordinated.
You must be robotic.
You must be a Machine.

Don't make a mistake.
Don't be sloppy.
Don't take a break.
Don't have a rest.
Don't slow down.
You must be a Machine.

This what we have been reduced to.
This is what we've become.
This is what our lives are.
This our world.
This is Humanity.
Welcome to The Machine.

"Welcome my friend.

Welcome, to....
.....the....
...... Machine!"

"The Don"
25.05.2020

Singularity

Robots.
Automotons
HuBots
Artificial Life forms.
Intelligent machines.
This is Singularity.

Humans becoming more like robots.
Robots becoming more like humans.
Human Robots are HuBots.
This is what we have become.
This is the Future
This is Singularity.

The merger of the machine & the human.
This is the future written by Isaac Asimov in "I Robot".
Predicted by Ray Kurzweil, so many years. ago.
Indistinguishable, becoming one & the same.
Unified, biological machines that can self-replicate & are sentient.
This is Singularity.

I love "Augmentation".
Bring it on.
The human body is a fragile vessel.
It needs to be improved.
Let's make it better.
I love Singularity.

Let's make it stronger.
Let's make it so that we can live longer.
Let's update it, it needs an upgrade.
Let's improve it & make it better.
Let's have a system overhaul.
Let's bring on Singularity.

Singularity is the way forward.
Singularity is the point of convergence.
Singularity is where a new human emerges.
Singularity is the birth of the New Human.
Singularity is beginning of "Human v2.0".
Singularity is the New Future Human.

Some have called it "H+".
Some have called it "Transhumanism'.
Some have called it "Going beyond the Human".
Some have called it "Transcendent Man".
Some have called it "The Man that Lives Forever".
I call it Singularity.

This is
Singularity

"The Don"
25.05.2020

Truth

Truth is a relative concept.
Truth is based on your point of view.
Truth is subjective.
Truth is not objective.
Truth is based on your perspective.
Truth is based on what coloured glasses you are wearing.
Truth is yours & yours only.
Truth is a LIE!

Truth can be bought & sold.
Truth is not justice.
Truth has many faces.
Truth is not worth fighting for.
Truth is not worth dying for.
Truth has caused many wars.
Truth has lost many battles.
Truth is not your friend.
Truth will let you down again & again.
Truth is FAKE!

Truth is an illusion.
Truth is a confusion.
Truth is a "game of bluff".
Truth is not the "Right Stuff".
Truth is a slap in your face.
Truth has destroyed the whole Human Race.
Truth is "pie in the sky".
Truth is "and pigs can fly".
Truth, you don't need to defend.
Truth is a DILUSION.

Truth lies straight to your face.
Truth is a misrepresentation.
Truth doesn't have just one voice.
Truth doesn't belong to one country or nation.
Truth is corrupt.
Truth is not to be trusted.
Truth doesn't exist.
Truth is "Chinese Whispers".
Truth can be contoured & distorted like a piece of string.
Truth is not to be believed.
Truth is a JOKE.

"And that is the TRUTH!"

"The Don"
26.05.2020

www.ingramcontent.com/pod-product-compliance
Lightning Source LLC
Chambersburg PA
CBHW041501010526
44107CB00049B/1616